frog's phone anxiety

and other poems

Brendan Ahern

© 2017 Brendan Ahern

All rights reserved.

This book contains material protected under International and Federal Copyright Laws and Treaties. Any unauthorized reprint or use of this material is prohibited. No part of this book may be reproduced or transmitted in any form or by any means, electronic or mechanical, including photocopying, recording, or by any information storage and retrieval system without express written permission from the author / publisher.

978-0-9958692-5-7

Published by Outside the Lines Press
Antigonish, Nova Scotia
www.outsidethelinespress.com

For retail and wholesale purchases of this book, contact the publisher via the above website.

"Thanks for the compost, idiots."
-fruit flies

Foreword

The Spring Peeper is a frog whose distinctive call can be interpreted as an incessant plea for the silent female of the species to "Please Have Sex With Me!".

There's a type of bird in Australia, the superb fairy wren, with an attractive bright blue head, and who presents yellow flower petals to the less colorful females, "Please Have Sex with Me!"

Some animals compete to build better nests, while others work to build stronger bodies than their competition.

And some animals get left out. Some don't eat enough, and get beaten by the alpha. Some, whose nests aren't up to scratch will find themselves living alone, while others might find that the bouquet has already been given. And, if you listen hard enough, you can hear a few spring peepers calling late into July. This one's for them.

-Brendan

Seal

You surface somewhere near,
close enough for me to count your whiskers.
Resting, as it looks to me,
in the way that I might rest with a cup of tea
on a Sunday afternoon.

How alike you and I must seem!
You, a seal.
And me, all wrapped-up
black and hooded in my neoprene skin
an imitation of your birthday suit.

Violin Beetle

The one who named you must have been a fan of the violin
Because you could have just as easily been a Cello Beatle.

It makes me wonder about your cousin
and the one who named it "Lady Bug".

I will never know who they had in mind,
but I can guess at how she used to dress.

Vulture

Before the battle, priests read the signs
inside the rooster's stomach.

And high above them, vulture waited
to eat what was still in theirs.

Lion

It would be strange to find a lion
resting in the Savannah
After having one tattooed on your sweaty shoulder.
From a zebra-striped safari jeep
you'd see its tail gently brushing away the flies.
Eyes half-lidded in the sun.

It would be enough to pull the rug out from anyone
who has recently had its likeness
inked orange and yellow,
and maybe green for those eyes that you described
as needing to be "bold"
on your tender human skin.

Bull Shark

If you wish to visit,
please call between 10 AM and 4 PM
because by then I will have already eaten my fill of hogfish.

They taste much better than you, but I'm not picky.
And, frankly, it is my house that you're playing in.
We don't want any more accidents.

Frog's Phone Anxiety

Steady rattle of rain
They wait out the rotten weather
In tiny tree-top apartments
where they sing the blues.
Like me,
cigarette in one hand,
phone in the other,
waiting for her to call me back.

Piping Plover

They have got to be some of the stupidest birds alive.
There, I said it.
They build their nests above the water-line
wherever the water-line happens to be on the day that they decide to build them.
It really doesn't take them long.
In fact, you'd get the same results if you lobbed a palm-sized stone into the sand,
and even that might exaggerate just how much these things excavate to incubate their children.
Who, by the way, are useless until they are able to reproduce.
At which time, they will no doubt copy their parents' behavior and build equally shitty nests.

White Tailed Deer

Typical

I can practically hear them say
just before they turn and run away,
white tails like warning signs
telling the others that,

*there's just another two-legged
treating the hill like a gym
or, worse still,
a zoo.*

Muskrat

Like the fool who sees the moon
and wonders if she can see it too,
I see a muskrat and think of You,
walking beside the river when I was swimming.

And if you're sick of sad love poems
if you've already rolled your eyes,
please know that I'm right there with you

a fly on the wall watching you read,
a moth in the closet hearing you speak,
a different muskrat on a different river
trying to be noticed.

Right Whale

like making a new friend
on the train

like finding money
on the sidewalk

like hearing your favorite song
on the radio,

Meeting you.

Apes

In the quest for fire their fingers burned
And among the flames in a conquest for food
One of them thought that, while they fought,
the water they brought
would be made a terrible waste.

Turtle

His house was full, with very little light
except for where it was needed to be.

And the walls were lined with wisdom
from all the corners of the world.

Tolkien's Fox

He means no harm
He's just passing by
But he has ears for hearing
He has eyes that can see
And he reminds us that something might be watching
wherever it is that you happen to be.
Like right now
Cooling my feet with the riverbank as my back-rest—
wet, brown and mossy
before giving-way to a far-green country.

I wonder what his fox would see
and try to act accordingly.

Tick

An old man in a big house lets the cat out each day at noon.
A young tick eagerly waits to wipe the smirk off the
spider's face.
"Hey, Hexapod", says the spider from her web in the old
man's window,
"you're no better than this blue bottle!"
and sticks a straw into her morning smoothie.

It is well understood within the scientific community
that spider taunts can make ticks reckless.
So, tick climbs the tall grass in an unmown portion of the
old man's yard
and snags the passing cat behind its ear,
burying herself face-first into a soft spot
with mouthparts like needle-nosed pliers.

Cat spends the day looking for squirrels
and tries to catch some birds
before returning home and jumping through
the open window where she ruins the spider's web.

Without noticing the growing tick, the old man goes to bed
and the happy tick drinks her fill
to the rhythm of a kitchen clock
counting everything down
one tic at a time.

www.ingramcontent.com/pod-product-compliance
Lightning Source LLC
Chambersburg PA
CBHW060458300426
44113CB00016B/2638